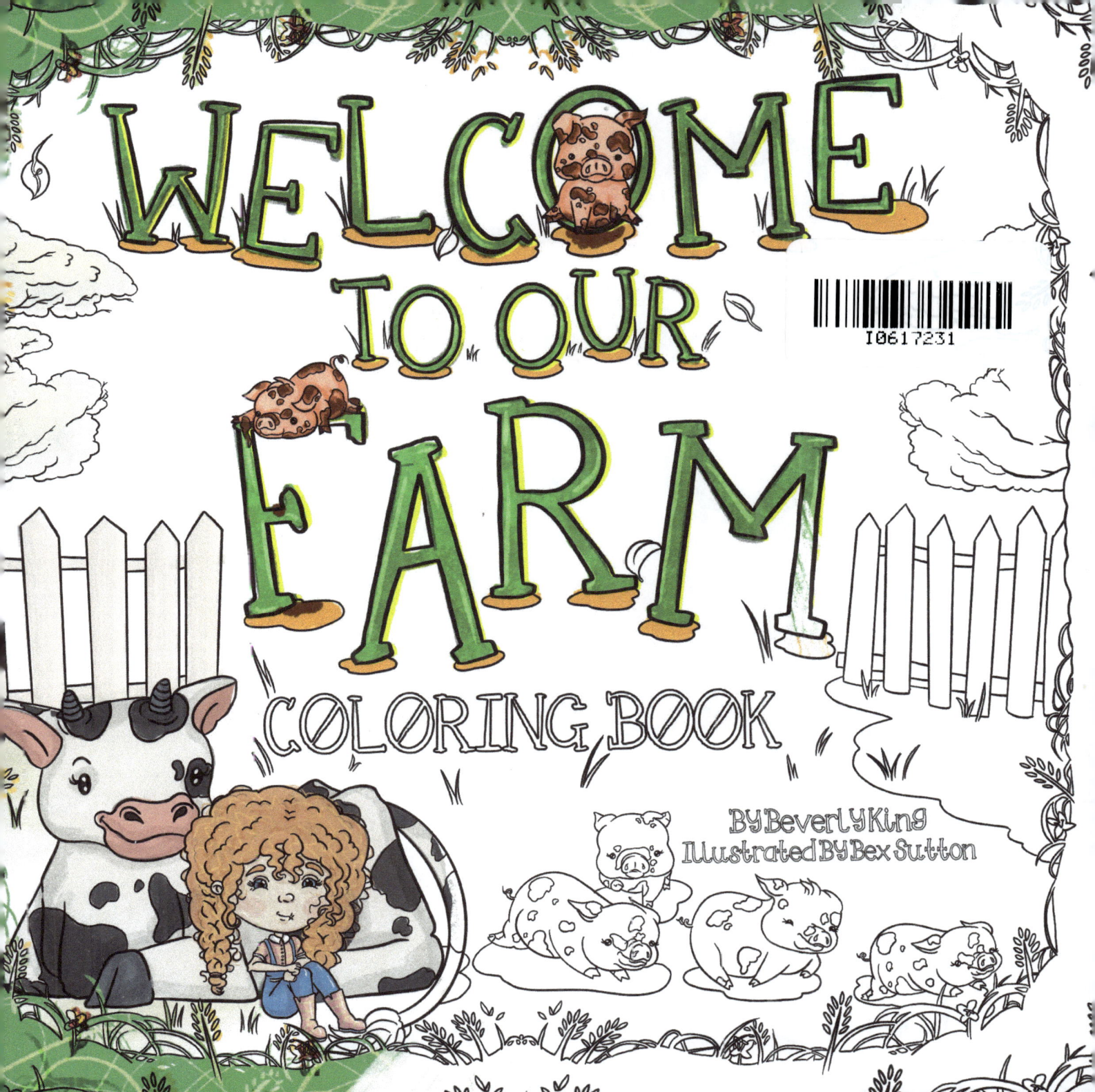

WELCOME TO OUR FARM

COLORING BOOK

BY Beverly King
Illustrated BY Bex Sutton

Find your
way through
the maze!
From one
side to the
other:

Find your
way out of
the center of
the maze!:

Find your
way out of
the center of
the maze!:

Find your way through the maze! From one side to the other: